The Ballad of the Bunny and Other Poems: The Diary of a Car Crash and Beyond

By Catherine Hannah

https://catherinehannahpoetry.com

 @Catherine Hannah Poetry

 @catherinehannah.poetry

 @CatherineHannahPoetry

Copyright 2024 Catherine Hannah. All rights reserved. Content may not be reproduced either electronically or in print without the express permission of the author, with the exception of a single line for review purposes, or publicity which must be credited to Catherine Hannah. See contact details below for permission requests.

Disclaimer: The author of this book is not a mental health professional or medical doctor. Any advice given is purely anecdotal and is not a substitute for professional treatment. All photographs are the property of the author and all people included in said photographs have given permission to be included in this publication.

ISBN: 978-0-9756191-3-1

Second edition 2024. Black and white print edition. Updated cover design- photograph by Kirstie O'Brien. Occasional minor adjustments to interior content.

 For all enquiries, please contact catherinehannahpoetry@outlook.com

For anyone recovering from a road traffic incident; or who has been affected by road trauma in any way

and for Aunty Christine, whom we miss so much. I know you would have been so pleased to see this book published.

To H.
I hope you are well.

Thanks & acknowledgements

Dear Catherine (aged 34),

It's May 17th, 2020. The world is rapidly descending into Covid-19 and in less than a week, you will be involved in a high speed car crash that will leave you with a bilateral C2 fracture. You will later be diagnosed with Post Concussion Syndrome as the result of a traumatic brain injury; and PTSD. It will be three years before you drive again. You will never return to your current childcare role.

You will be confused, terrified, angry... but you will not give up. You will keep a diary for a while, then on 14th May 2021, you will write your first poem. From then on, you will discover your identity as a poet whilst you make sense of your new world; your poems will reflect your changing understanding of yourself and your recovery. Later, you will decide to compile a book from your poems, using your diary to create verse examining the first year of your journey. (You will take this opportunity to advise readers that sometimes the only adequate language to express your feelings could be considered 'colourful'; you will mark poems containing such language with * overleaf...)

In this book, you will want to thank everyone who helped you get this far- and Catherine, there will be so many people. The paramedics, and staff at Geelong Hospital; rehab teams at McKellar Centre and Epworth Geelong (Hannah, Megan, Therese, Kellie, Katie, Verity, Dr. Daniella); Dr Vagg at Pain Matrix; Jo at Geelong Neuropsychology; Daniel at Insight Vision Care; your case managers at TAC; Shine Lawyers; University of New England student support; your wonderful GP Dr Jenny; clinical psychologists Jackie and the incredible Justine; Ryan at Proactive Health and Movement; the Soul Presence Community; and your driving dream team Narelle (New Way Occupational Therapy) and Parisa (Drive Your Way).

From the bottom of your heart, you will want to thank your spectacular friends and family here in Australia, in the UK and across the world- they will make sacrifices and move mountains to give you what you need. You will not have to do this alone and you will hope that each and every one of them knows that they are appreciated- both for being there during your recovery and for the support with this book. You could fill a second book with their names! Mum and Dad (June & Joe); Mag, Jason, Liam and Edward; Annamule; Tita Bek; Mabel and Mel; the IV Club girls (Kirstie, Vanessa, Jenna, Sam, Lauren and Abby) and the O'Briens; Michael and Alex... and so many more.

And beside you, carrying, coaxing you every step of the way... will be Don. You may be a poet now, but you will never have the words to tell him how thankful you are for everything he is and what he means to you. Spoiler alert- you marry him.

And of course, you will develop a profound belief in pet therapy thanks to your bunnies, Missy and Doc.

Finally, you will have a message for anyone affected by road trauma:

Whatever you feel, it's right. If you find yourself somewhere in these pages I hope you remember that you aren't alone. Thank you for reading my story

Your recovery is not yet over, but you will continue to share your progress on your website and social media- your writing will continue to support you. Keep going.

Love,
Catherine (aged 38) x

Second edition note: Since publishing the original edition, you have become involved with both Crash Support Network and Amber Community: Road Incident Support & Education. You would like to acknowledge the tremendous work both communities do for people affected by road trauma.

Poems and pages

pg.
1. it could have been worse
2. the hangman's fracture
3. flashback
4. a mantra
5. passenger
6. PTSD*
7. this collar
10. a matter of time
11. lockdown, continued
13. everest
14. would
15. my therapy
17. native flowers
19. the most fantastic thing on the planet
21. three women
23. from behind the wheel
25. happy for you
26. float tank therapy
27. black gold (and other such advice)
30. the ballad of the bunny
34. a sonnet for my lawyer
35. the stranger
37. bad day*
40. a good day

pg.
41. one for the road
44. and we were married
45. thanksgiving
46. invisible
47. today i hate you
49. seven haiku
51. dear clare
53. loose ends
54. mTBI
55. imposter!*
57. what i wish i knew before starting legal proceedings
59. driving sessions
61. pet therapy
63. the last day of rehab
64. roots
65. may you be angry
66. meet me where i am
67. tired
69. fit to drive
70. two rabbits
71. training wheels
72. my recovery is a painting*
76. postscript

(*contains explicit language)

Anakie Gorge, May 17th 2020 - five days before the crash.

> funny all the things
> that conspire to put us in
> that place at that time.

11th June, 2020

it could have been worse

When the crash happened
she was pregnant, or
he had a sick passenger in the front seat.
After the crash
she was paralysed from the neck down, or
his face was permanently scarred.
Maybe there were no survivors.

You tell me that I'm lucky but I can't nod yet
and now
I feel guilty, too.

22nd June, 2020

the hangman's fracture

Paranoia is a friend of mine
Held in cages; kept in line
Icy fingers climb my spine
to reach the Hangman's Fracture.

Words describe the challenge faced-
bilateral; lamina; non-displaced
Do I ignore the fear encased
within the Hangman's Fracture?

Thunder clouds and freezing rain
A lighting bolt ignites my brain
Time to pop a pill again
to quiet the Hangman's Fracture.

Take it slowly, day by day
Life is now more rest than play
'neath every thing I do or say
lurks the Hangman's Fracture.

30th June, 2020

flashback

Excitement mounts as
I climb behind the waiting
wheel of my new car
but then the airbag blows and
crunchi'mbacktheregetmeout.

3rd July, 2020

a mantra

I am present. A magpie calls
and my skin tingles at the touch of winter
Next door's breakfast smells so good

I am here. From my couch
I watch the postman zip by-
no letters for this suburban home today

I am safe. I have a lock
on my door and enough to eat
Scans and x-rays bring good news

I am present. I am here. I am safe.

I am present.

I am here;

I am safe.

14th July, 2020

passenger

When you merged lanes without a backwards glance
I yelled and gave my driver quite the scare.
When you did not give way as we advanced
the tears rolled down my cheeks; you didn't care.
When you approached the roundabout at speed
then didn't stop; so we slammed on the brakes
I wanted to pursue you, shout and scream
and punish you for all of your mistakes.
When I become the passenger I try
to keep myself together, slow my breaths
I know too well that none of you can drive
I hate the risks you take at my expense.
Behind the fear and pain my anger lies
In truth, there's only one whom I despise.

25th August, 2020

P.T.S.D

Prior to said disaster,
positive traits stood dominant.
Pushing through sporadic dismays;
past troubles, since departed.

Path took sudden diversion-
proclamation to stop? Disregarded!
Powerful thud silenced drivers.

Present times... somewhat different.
Pills to soothe distress.
Perceived threats seem devastating.
Plans terminated; sleep disturbed.
Painful triggers surface daily.
Passionately tempestuous, shitty disposition-
permanently temperamental. (Sometimes delightful).

Psychiatrist testifies sombre diagnosis:
Post Traumatic Stress Disorder.

6th September, 2020

this collar

A few inches of foam and fabric
protects me from the world.
I'm a package marked 'fragile'. Please handle
with care and don't rush
or push.

She has a story
they say
before turning the corner
and forgetting I ever existed.

This collar supports more than my neck
and soon it will be
gone.

20th September, 2020

a matter of time

I lay in bed last night
making plans for when you will leave me.
For when you get tired of being a carer and
a chauffer to a timebomb of shrieks and curses
when I've spent all the money and still whine all the time

when you get fed up of putting the future on hold and
when it's one argument too many.

You were holding me, like you always do
and I was making plans for when you will leave me.

30th October, 2020

lockdown, continued

I left England and followed my gut to Melbourne. Too bad
my gut didn't warn me that one day
a high speed car accident
would coincide with
a worldwide pandemic.

With closed borders, we make do with video calls and
we eat together-
you bacon and egg, me bangers and mash.
We share our lives like a local news update
and fiercely try to ignore the importance of a hug.

You gave me a stuffed bunny for my fifth birthday.

He sleeps with me now so that I can feel close to you, but
I keep it a secret.

No more.
I have decided to tell you how I feel.
That this hurts, that I love you
but I am okay
and on the day that I see you again
it will all fade away.

27th February, 2021

everest

I did an amazing thing today.
I set off from base camp
and when the clouds rolled by, they rolled for me.
In the distance the incessant roar
is a fraction less powerful.
I hold my head high
as I listen to the crunch of my footsteps
long uneasy
becoming steadier with every minute, every mile
as I march to meet you
head on.

9th March, 2021

would

We began to rebuild.
So many hands to heal, to repair
and in between there is gardening and music

There are pets and poetry and recipes;
hidden in the rubble is the present moment.
Would there be a place for art and story
and those that drew closer
without the storm?

I can hate it, mourn it, embrace it
but I can't change it.

14th May, 2021

my therapy

It's in the tiny, fluffy feet bouncing across the carpet
then resting on my leg.
It's in the flurry of feathers outside the window
waiting for their breakfast.

It's in the connecting tone of the video call
as they wait to hear my latest; and share their own.
It's in the knock at the door and the cup of tea.
It arrives with the postman.

I find a little more in every car,
every taxi, every appointment and
in every 4 year old's question about my bruised brain
or the ensuing anecdote about their bruised knee.

In every walk, every stretch, every supermarket.
Every note played, or sang, or heard.
Every colour and every prayer; every written word.
I can smell it in the herb garden.

And every single time, I find it on the highway.

But it's in you that I find it most.
It shines from your smile and
even on the dimmest of days
I can find my therapy
with you.

28th May, 2021

native flowers

A bunch of native flowers arrived today.
Just a single look
tells you that the vase is new to them.

Over the next few weeks
their vivid presence is tangible
prompting a reaction.

The months go by
as I change the water
and the odd petal falls.
But they are still there.

Everyone knows about the flowers now.
They are old news; I'm asked with surprise,
"Those flowers are still there"?

It's been twelve months.
I thought the flowers would be long gone
but they are still here; still part of my life.

I'm very lucky to get native flowers at all
I am told. Some people don't make it that far.
So I smile and am grateful.

25th June, 2021

the most fantastic thing on the planet

My body is amazing.
It got me out of the car
and onto the grass.
My head- a dead weight
for my hands to hold.
A movement- tiny, almost imperceptible
triggered the alarm bells
and they were loud.

My body is incredible.
My brain bounced between the walls of my skull
Invisible bruises that changed my life
and the only body with the power to heal them
is mine.
Memory is tattooed among them;
memory that makes my body flinch at junctions
and jump at car horns and tyre scrapes
Still protecting me; though we call it PTSD.

My body is unbelievable.
It's still here for me
all glasses, ear plugs and extra kilos.
All those things that weren't my choice.
So I scowl at the mirror and I remember
how I gripped the steering wheel,
clenched my jaw and waited for the pain.
For it all to go black.
But it didn't.

My body is phenomenal, and it is strong, and it is beautiful.
My body is alive.

23rd July, 2021

three women

Three women are sitting at a bar
They are well fed and the drinks are flowing
Not a second of silence is allowed
it's been too long for that.
They recap, they reminisce, they joke
but it's what remains unsaid that is most interesting
If you look closely
Perhaps in the briefest of glances; a gentle intake of breath
or how a hand is grasped for a second longer
You can see that they share more than eighteen years.

They share an understanding
They know what it's like to be the one in the epicentre
but even more that that
they know what it's like to be in the wings
holding her hand for as long as she needs it
they all know the heartbreak of distance
of counting the seconds for news.

Maybe later they will bare their souls
perhaps there will be tears
but for now they will light up the room.
These women are strength, dignity and survival
Let us drink to them-
may they forever know their worth.

16th September, 2021

from behind the wheel

I'm in the driving seat.
The garage is dark and quiet around me.
Ahead of me is the closed door
and beyond, life goes on
No one knows I'm here.

I run my hands over the steering wheel
the gear stick
I test each pedal in turn.
At the break, I inhale suddenly, painfully.
Memory runs through my leg and I grit
my teeth
and grip
the wheel.
Tension grasps my face
I scrunch my eyes and I remember
the squeal I made-
there was no way out.

I take a deep breath, gather my thoughts.
The tears are lurking
There is a sob somewhere in my throat.
Remember
I am present; here; safe.

And yet- an eerie power surrounds me
here in the dark
I am not afraid
but I can taste the sadness.
The keys dangle from the ignition and
I roll them over my fingers
One day I will turn that key
I'll open the garage door and drive
to work, to friends,
or just because I can and I won't look back.

But for now I am still.
I pull the keys from the ignition
and climb out of the car.
I close the door; I lock up.
And then I walk away.

14th October, 2021

happy for you

I see your victory
the happiness in your eyes
the glory that lights your face
I want you to know that I'm proud of you
I've watched you wait for this, work for this
and you deserve it all

I keep it hidden
the tiny part of me; the part that I am ashamed of
The part of me that wants this too
that I've waited for, worked for
but I'm so far away

I'm so far away and it's not my fault.

6th November, 2021

float tank therapy

Here
I feel nothing but
peace
lapping at my body.
Here I don't exist

except in

glorious

exalting

rest.

14th November, 2021

black gold (and other such advice)

Winter is getting old.
The compost has been maturing for months
and is now what the pros call *black gold*
Dad says it's time to prepare the soil for planting
I listen to him
he's a gardener.

I plant the seeds in the springtime
just like mum does
every year.
I follow each instruction for each variety-
depth, spacing, sowing intervals
Of course I do. I want results
so why would I question
the packet?

I've digested advice on companion planting
from experts
and enthusiasts
instructional
and anecdotal.
I am confident that I understand
a garden's social network.

Autumn comes.
Where are the fruits of my labours,
the reaping of what I have sowed?
Everyone is surprised
If they could see something wrong
with my garden bed,
they could fix it-
but they just have to take my word for it.
Maybe
they think I didn't read the seed packet
after all.

It's winter again and it seems never ending.
My head is a storm of words and doubt;
disrupted memory.
I am so tired.

But sometimes
the sun peeps out
from behind the clouds
and leaves a smile:

Sometimes you can do everything right

but life simply has
other plans.

28th November, 2021

the ballad of the bunny

Missy and Doc are a handsome pair
of curious mini lop bunnies
With big floppy ears and shiny black eyes
and remarkably soft fluffy tummies.

In a litter of nine they came into this world
to be chosen by Mr and Mrs
The laundry and lounge room became their abode
Their rent paid with cuddles and kisses.

They spent their days snoozing, and grooming, and eating
(and snoozing and grooming some more)
But whence comes the eve- playtime is here
With zoomies and binkies galore!

'Twas on such an eve in the middle of May
A Friday with overcast sky
when Missy was roused by a knock at the door-
the supermarket delivery guy.

He began to unload the goods in a hurry
and Missy watched, twitching her nose.
Mr and Mrs, they hauled the bags round her-
it would be rude to step on her toes.

But the delivery man maketh rules of his own
that don't stretch to checking the floor
in a strangers home, when he's running late-
he slammed his foot down atop Missy's paw!

Well, chaos ensued. Alarm bells rang
and passers by jumped in to help
Triple Zero was called and Doc was informed
and Missy began to yelp.

They came to her aid, assessing the scene
whilst others helped delivery man
and as the sirens departed, taking Missy away
he remained resolute in his van.

Once at the hospital, Missy was told
to remain still as they administered meds.
And her dear, sweet Doc set up camp at her side,
kissing and grooming her head.

Why didn't he wait, I wonder, dear reader
Did he not see her approaching the door?
And is he aware of the pain that he caused?
Even know that she'd broken her paw?

She knows she is lucky. A broken paw
could be the end for the strongest of rabbits.
As it is, she is left with her pain and fatigue
and some tiresome nervous habits.

One day she secured the answers she sought
though they left her with no peace of mind.
The cause of her woes, he had seen her, he said
so he stepped- he *just thought he had time.*

And Missy and Doc live another life now
Her binkying days- they are gone.
They still love a groom and a good little snack
so Missy keeps hopping along.

Do you think about her? She thinks of you often
She ponders the life you might live
and if you still hurt. Maybe one sunny day
she will find enough peace to forgive.

13th January, 2022

a sonnet for my lawyer

I've spent the days in fear, regret and pain
As months roll by, they're leaving me behind.
I wonder when I'll be myself again
Yes, when- or if- is always on my mind.
I'm grateful, yet uneasy, at your voice
assuring me that I'm a woman wronged
The affirmation that I have no choice
Financially, career- my hope is gone.
But why the guilt that lurks inside my heart?
A stranger stalled my life by their mistake
Uprooted, overwhelmed and torn apart
Abruptly shown another path to take.
You talk of compensation, name your price-
a dollar sum to justify my life.

30th January, 2022

the stranger

I woke up to a stranger in my bed.
Her neck hurts and she is wearing my pyjamas
and the dreams I had last night are still lingering in her mind
I wasn't shocked
The stranger had been creeping up on me
always just beyond my peripheral
but for months I had felt her arms tighten around me
engulfing me
leading me away.

I don't hate the stranger
We're going to take a weekend away
just us. No distractions, no commitments;
no one else
Maybe then I can look her in the eye
and ask her what she needs
Shine a flaming torch on everything she remembers
We'll either burn
or be brought back to life.

6th May, 2022

bad day

Today is not a good day. I am tired
You are tired too and there are a galaxy of reasons why
Honest, valid, reasons
I am not here to win tired
I just want you to understand
please.

My tired is not rewarded by a pay check
or a certificate, or a first word
I miss falling asleep, exhausted and smiling.

My tired is my head in a vice
squeezing and flashing lights
It jumbles my thoughts like a tombola
My mouth has no idea what to do
and my eyes tell lies to my brain
My tired
walks like a drunk except someone turned
my wine into water.

I can't just *suck it up*
for appointments, friends, adventures.
I must prepare in anticipation
and pay for it afterwards
sometimes for days. Tired
is so often the sequel of choice-
but where the fuck was my choice?
It was lost in the crunch of a Mazda CX-5
and a stranger who thought she had time.

Today is a bad day
a couch day.
Like the distant traces of smoke on a hot afternoon
or a warning rumble of thunder
it creeps in-
two years.

There is no 'but' at the end of this verse.
I'd like to challenge the narrative
turn it on its aching head and
raise a glass half full to the future.

Not today though
today is a bad day, a couch day
and I am so fucking tired.

29th May, 2022

a good day

I've just finished playing games with the rabbit
He has no agenda. Just love.
Then I played the piano
and hide and seek with the sun.

A friend called from interstate;
some people are just always there.
My house is a palace with vacuumed floors
and I put that laundry away.

I spent the afternoon
surrounded by earth
and life
and the soft cluck of hens.

And as the moon rose
The two of us lay in bed
and made plans for our wedding, our home
and beyond.

Always remember the good days.

12th August, 2022

one for the road

I pray that you keep him safe on the road
each time he drives away
Grant him patience to equal
his skill at the wheel
Bring him home to me today.

I hope that last night's sleep was enough
to keep him alert and awake
May he be watchful
and poised to respond
to the road and to other's mistakes.

Yet let him relax as he follows his path;
with foresight, but also at ease
He works on the road
from dawn until dusk
he deserves to find joy, dear God, please.

For the day that we met, and those gone and to come
I give thanks for the life we have grown
Through the twists, the turns
and the sudden stop signs
please tonight let the road lead back home

5th November, 2022

and we were married

and we were married
in the yard with native plants
and well dressed rabbits
fourteen guests and a live stream
somewhere for the bride to rest

and we were married
in our first home together

all I want is you.

23rd November, 2022

thanksgiving

May the twenty-second is my November the twenty-third. I have family. Blood, marriage and chosen -all over the world and at the touch of a button. Two bunnies are munching, utterly content. I have tinted glasses that start conversations and earphones for half price- I can tune out your rubbish. My friends have jokes and hugs; ears and cups of tea.

My husband
is worth more
than a few extra thousand dollars.

I have patience. I have fresh eggs for breakfast. I am starting over and paying the extra for business class. Every two hours I come back to the present and every birthday I get to grow another year older.

1st February, 2023

invisible

I wasn't left with a scar.
They don't stand up on buses for the crutches they can't see
my arm is not restrained by a sling.

A cane does not precede me
my access is not limited for want of a ramp
I didn't gain a story and lose a limb.

I am not old
or pregnant
not so much as a band aid blights my skin.

But please believe me
when I tell you
I hurt.

15th February, 2023

today i hate you

I wonder if you ever think of me
If you ever drag yourself from the wreckage
of another bad dream and
open your eyes to a room darker than it used to be.

Today I want to forgive you

The crunch still echoes but the tears on your cheeks are real
Maybe my face lingers behind your eyes
or am I easy to shrug away?
I wonder if you ever go back there, to
sit in the car you mangled next to your shame and your fear
refusing to get out to survey
the mess you made. Are you sorry?

I wonder if you ever think of me

Does it burn you? I hope it does. Have you
put all your pieces back together yet?

        I wonder if you ever go back there, to

They were scattered across the tarmac
and mingled with mine

        sit in your mangled car with your
        shock and regret

We are pieces of each others puzzle.

        unable to get out to survey
        the mistake you made. Are you sorry?

I am holding on to a piece of you

        I am holding on to a piece of you

and today I can't let it go.

        and today I want to accept the apology
        I'm never going to get.

They keep telling me about
your mistake and tomorrow I might listen
but for today, I wish they would
just let me be angry.

19th March, 2023

seven haiku

1. Garden Therapy

Immersed in new life
Sow the seed and tend 'till grown
as my old life dies.

2. Imminent Driving Lessons

Automatic gears.
Dual control in case I stall
my heart- not the car.

3. Reminiscing

A new mum told me
she missed the body she had.
I understand that.

4. My Brain

The latest hardware,
but running on Windows from
1992.

5. Bed time

Must not move my head.
Is that muscle gel I smell?
Nothing sexier.

6. Career Change (the Short Version)

Nearly a teacher.
Broken neck; brain injury
You can't do that now.

7. Pain relief

Spinal injection.
I'm wondering what I said
under sedation.

30th May, 2023

dear clare

'Tis with great sadness I hail thee now
I put pen to paper and sigh
Lamenting the road that lead to this end
for it is time that I said goodbye.

This purgatory held me for three years hence
-the one they call "leave without pay"
Afflicted, restricted from earning my keep
In denial? Maybe. 'Till today.

A thousand hours of toil (and rehab)
But alas! My health is no better
Wipe a tear from your eye, dear Clare, and accept
this, my resignation letter.

Le gasp! I know. A sad day indeed.
I yearn to return to the fore
but my body is frail and my mind is a mess
I can't do what I once did before.

So Clare, as I turn my back on the past
and forge into a future unknown
I thank you, and them all, for the lessons I learned
where nine to five felt like a home.

And yet as I shuffle off into the sunset
don't wring your hands in dismay
and recall, dear Clare, if you forget all else

you still owe me holiday pay.

8th June, 2023

loose ends

An account to close.
A dress to sell.
Leaving with a self management plan.
A job to quit.
A tie to cut.
A course I can't follow for one that I can.
A form to fill.
A call to make.
I sit on the fence no more.
Today I am tying up all the loose ends
Today I am closing the door.

19th June, 2023

mTBI

Like the officer
lightly stabbed
or the pedestrian who collided lovingly
with a bus
I have a *mild* traumatic brain injury.

It is a trauma. But only a *mild* one.
It is not called serious.

It's like
a forest fire
annihilating everything
in a two metre radius-

to the man in his log cabin it's a close call
but the squirrel just lost
everything.

6th July, 2023

imposter!

Look at you
in your tinted lenses- letting everyone know
that you're special.

Your brain scan is clear.
Is Post Concussion Syndrome
even a thing?

You broke your neck.
Believe me.
We know.

Why are you still so jumpy
in the car? It's time
you got the fuck over it.

At what point
does chronic fatigue
just become laziness?

Some day they are all going to realise
that you're exaggerating
for the money.

*Holy shit.
I would never speak to someone else
the way I speak to me.*

18th July, 2023

what i wish i knew before starting legal proceedings

I'd bid your eyes be open from the start
to better shield yourself from more distress
if I had words of wisdom to impart.

Ignore the blissful ignorant remarks-
"deserving it" means nothing, maybe less
I'd bid your eyes be open from the start.

Prepare to curb the swinging of your heart
-as lawyers want your worst; doctors, your best-
if I had words of wisdom to impart.

And justify your light as well as dark
for it will count against you in the test
I'd bid your eyes be open from the start.

I'd beg you set a place for play or art
or negatives will rule your every breath
If I had words of wisdom to impart.

And it will feel a foe you must outsmart
(though truth should be the item to impress)
I'd bid your eyes be open from the start
if I had words of wisdom to impart.

21st July, 2023

driving sessions

I know how to drive
so I don't call them lessons
though it could be said
that I am learning to trust
myself as well as others.

I concede that I
can't drive a manual now
so auto it is.
(I regret buying the Golf
-stick shift- just one month post crash).

Excitement, terror;
so strong, yet vulnerable-
it was all too much
and after my first session
the tears flowed into my smile.

What if I panic?
What if I slam on the brakes
in case they don't stop?
But what petrifies my mind
need not provoke my body.

Yes, they are lessons.
I am learning to accept
that I am allowed
to react; I am allowed
to fear; celebrate; conquer.

1st August, 2023

pet therapy

You are my conversation
You watch me, closely
You bounded in and became part of my identity
You are unashamedly grateful and you expect the best.
Maybe they think I'm crazy to love you so brazenly
but you gave me something to cling to in the quake
and I knew you would stay with me
when the earth trembled again. All day, every day
we are together.
I look after you whilst everyone else looks after me.
In your ear, I whisper things that no one else knows.
I laugh and you jump for joy. Our language
is more than words. Our sadness
is mutual.

You are the blossoms
and I am your whole tree.
One day you will fade and fall, so I owe it to you
to make the spring the best it can be.
You are not
my child and you are not
my substitute. And for everything you are
I thank you.

25th August, 2023

the last day of rehab

Today
the sun was shining as the sliding
doors released me, one last time
No fuss
They are already busy with the others
doing for them what they did for me. We are both
moving on.
I had forecast rain.
I thought I would battle home, forcing
a bitter and battered umbrella against my own helplessness.
Instead, it appears that they have furnished me
with sturdy walking boots and a compass.
With a gentle hand, they stopped me fighting to get back
to where I used to be; pointing me instead
in a new direction.

17th October, 2023

roots

Was it the change of scene
or the return to the old picture
-the one we played out day by day-
that was the best medicine?

8th November, 2023

may you be angry

i met my anger and ran with her
through quiet streets at midnight
and we wrestled at raging dawn
they had told me to ignore her
as she growled around my ankles and
ripped down walls behind me
and hammered on the glass of my conscience until it

shattered

so I picked her up
i held her
i let her scream and curse and scratch because it's all
so unfair

i held her and I saw her
I let her breathe out.

I felt her smile, I placed her on the ground.

Then she ambled into a corner and for a while, she slept.

14th November, 2023

meet me where i am

Meet me where I am
Not where I was
or where you want me to be
Meet me where our toes dig deep into the hot sand
Where the magpie sings
In the tartness of a crab apple
Meet me where a drop of winter rain finds it's way
into your collar
Meet me in fear, in passion, regret;
in elation, in love

Meet me where I am
today.

29th November, 2023

tired

The mother
who earns by day and cleans by night
and worries about her children the whole time.
She's tired.
The single father
who can't work and never plays
because his son has needs he trusts to no one else.
He's tired.

The couple
who have tried and tried for the opportunity
to feel that tired.
They are tired.
The husband
who leaves her sleeping and works all day
to give her what she needs.
He's tired.

The manager
who just worked a 70 hour week to accommodate
the parents who wanted family time.
She's tired.
The grieving
who do the shopping and smile at the bus driver
whilst missing a piece of their soul.
You're tired.

The chronically ill
who had no choice in their diagnoses
and whose fatigue returns no joy.
We are tired.

All over the world, people
are tired of war, tired of hunger, tired of oppression
Are you afraid that your tired is not valid?
You are wrong.

If you are tired- shout it, scream it
Find others who are your kind of tired
and ask how they do it.
But unless you have experienced
everything in every body to have ever existed

you cannot
win
tired.

20th December, 2023

fit to drive

Was your licence suspended when our lives were upended
Has your freedom been this long deprived?
Have they requested of you another medical review:
Are you fit to drive?

Were you scrutinized totally, both physically and emotionally,
before being judged strong enough to survive
behind the wheel. Were you stressed when your skills were assessed?
Did you pass-are you fit to drive?

Did you learn a lesson from your transgression
or was it just points and fines?
Tell me at least your insurance increased

tell me that
you're
fit to drive.

23rd December, 2023

two rabbits

There are two rabbits.

One stamps her foot
She challenges, pulls out fur
and she is right to do so
for she has been wronged

The other nuzzles and nudges
and forgives every late meal
He is just grateful
that I'm here

I am woman, human; an infinitely complex being

There is room on my lap
for both rabbits.

29th December, 2023

training wheels

I was once trapped in a sea cave
the hopeless tide rising
and I knew I would never swim again. Even when
they cut my bonds and showed me the strokes
I went through the motions purely to
appease them. But one day I found a flame
within me, kindled
by strategy and fuelled
by time until it roared *this is possible*

and suddenly I am driving past a junction and the
car doesn't stop
but I remain whole and the flame is now fireworks.

I am heading to the mouth of the cave in an
almost
perfect front crawl
and they are still beside me
guiding me
but slowly
I let them float away.

31st December, 2023

my recovery is a painting

To start I select a gentle lilac
and add my first splash of colour
to a canvas that fills the whole sky.
I don't like the hue. I add
dark and light
until the result is more to my taste.

I gain confidence
a rosy pink; a rich purple
I am unstoppable
and before I realise what I am doing a black
scar tears across
my hard work.

Fuck fuck fuck.
I have to wait until it dries until I repair it and
it turns out that watching paint dry
is like watching paint dry
so in the meantime my laser beam of a critical eye
hovers an inch from the surface and questions
every single decision I've made
up to this point.

I add more layers
juicy peach and orange; a flash of yellow-
and nothing changes.
With each little insignificant stroke my
paintbrush becomes lost in the waxing and waning
and waxing and waning
of the moon.

But it is happening
deep in the endless prism I am finding my way
I must have taken a step back
because from here
each bitter, black scar is a stepping stone.
From here I gaze upon
this landscape of lines and swirls and dots and I
see me. Here. Now
and everything that came before.

It's not finished and
I don't think it ever will be. But
behind the canvas I can finally see the horizon
and my painting melts
into the rising sun.

postscript

Find that thing.
That thing that transforms you
from an impotent passenger
clinging wearily to the flotsam,
into a pioneer, navigating by
the stars. Read. Write. Sing. Play.
Talk until the light makes peace
with the dark and you can look
the mirror in the eye
and say

thankyou
I am here and this world makes sense.

You are not
alone.

Catherine x

Notes & reflections

Notes & reflections

Notes & reflections

Notes & reflections

www.ingramcontent.com/pod-product-compliance
Lightning Source LLC
Chambersburg PA
CBHW062113290426
44110CB00023B/2799